SAM SHERRATT PUBLIC
649 LAURIER AVENUE
MILTON, ONTARIO
L9T 4N4

MW01323855

KARATE

TERENCE O'RORKE

Wayland

GO FOR SPORT!: KARATE

Go For Sport!
Basketball
Cricket
Fishing
Gymnastics
Judo
Karate
Rugby
Soccer

Cover: Former British and world karate champion Vic Charles.

Acknowledgements
Many thanks to Vince Morris of the English Karate Governing Body for his invaluable knowledge and advice, and to John Gichigi, who took many of the photographs used in this book.

Picture acknowledgements
The publishers would like to thank the following for providing the photographs used in this book: Allsport 5 (Gerard Planchenault/Vandystadt), 6 (Bruno Bade/Vandystadt), 7 (David Lean), 11 (Yann Guichaoua/Vandystadt), 13, 14, 15, 20, 21, 22, 23, 24, 26, 27, 28, 36, 37, 38, 39 (all John Gichigi), 43 (Yann Guichaoua/Vandystadt); Sylvio Dokov 9, 10, 18, 25, 31, 32, 33, 34, 35, 44, 45.

Series Editor: James Kerr
Designer: Malcolm Walker

First published in 1994 by
Wayland (Publishers) Limited,
61 Western Road,
Hove, East Sussex, BN3 1JD

© Copyright 1994 Wayland (Publishers) Limited

British Library Cataloguing in Publication Data
O'Rorke, Terence
  Karate - (Go for Sport! Series)
  I. Title II. Series
  796.8

ISBN 0-7502-0788-4

Typeset by Kudos Editorial and Design Services
Printed and bound in Italy by G.Canale and C.S.p.A.

Contents

INTRODUCTION 4
HISTORY AND DEVELOPMENT 6
GETTING STARTED 11
TECHNIQUES 1 19
TECHNIQUES 2 24
TECHNIQUES 3 35
GLOSSARY 46
FURTHER READING 47
USEFUL ADDRESSES 47
INDEX 48

INTRODUCTION

Karate is one of the best-known and most practised fighting arts in the world today. It is an effective means of self-defence, as well as an enjoyable combat sport, an excellent way of keeping fit, and a worthwhile form of self-discipline.

Karate has become very popular in the last few decades because it allows people of all ages and both sexes to take part. There are no restrictions based on size and ability, and the sport can be adapted to meet individual needs.

If you decide to take up karate, be prepared to work hard. In order to master the movements you need to be fit and supple, so do not go into it half-heartedly.

Combat karate involves fighting against someone of the same sex and of a similar size. Some people enjoy this, while others prefer to concentrate on the non-contact side. Competition karate is optional in most clubs, so do not be put off by the thought of having to 'fight' all the time.

There are many different forms of karate. The most popular style is shotokan, though in this book we shall look at some of the techniques that are common to most styles.

It is not possible to learn the sport merely by reading this book, and you should make sure that you get the correct tuition. Also, karate can be

Karate is one of the most spectacular fighting arts.

a very dangerous sport, and you should not practise without the supervision of a trained instructor.

Remember, karate is a form of self-defence and a disciplined way of keeping fit. You should take it up for these reasons – not to be the toughest in your school!

HISTORY AND DEVELOPMENT

Though the origins of karate go back more than 1,400 years, the styles that are practised today are relatively modern. It is believed that karate originated from a form of yoga developed by the Buddhist monk Bhodidharma. However, it was not until the twentieth century that the forms of karate we know today were established.

In the fifth century AD, Bhodidharma travelled from an area in

Former British and world karate champion Vic Charles.

Many people enjoy karate because it not only teaches self-defence and discipline, but it is also an excellent way of keeping fit.

northern India to teach at the Shaolin monastery in China. His yoga, which was designed to give enlightenment of the body and mind, was combined with a form of fighting called 'kempo' to help the Shaolin monks in their religious battles. They soon became well known for their courage and strength, and it wasn't long before the techniques spread to nearby areas.

Okinawa, an island just off Japan, was one of the first places to adopt the new style. The inhabitants, who were prohibited from carrying weapons, already had their own form of fighting, called 'te', and they blended this with the Shaolin methods to create 'Okinawa-te' – the immediate forerunner of modern-day karate.

Over the years the combination of Chinese and Japanese fighting styles became more and more effective, and the peasants were able to use the techniques in their unarmed battles against the Japanese warlords.

Towards the end of the nineteenth century, relations between Japan and Okinawa improved, and in 1922 the Japanese navy requested a demonstration of the impressive fighting technique. A schoolteacher by the name of Gichin Funakoshi was chosen to give the display. His presentation was so well received that, when he was invited back, he decided to resign from his job and become a full-time martial arts instructor.

This form had long been called karate, kara meaning 'China', and te 'hands', so the literal meaning was 'China-hands'. Kara also means 'empty' if spelled differently, and Mr Funakoshi changed the same-sounding word to mean 'empty-hands' or 'unarmed-hands'.

The karate style invented by Funakoshi is called shotokan, and has become the best-known and most popular style in the world today. However, due to the upswing in popularity of karate in Japan, other masters were attracted from Okinawa and China to give instructions to Funakoshi's students, who by then had become masters in their own right.

Other popular styles include shito-ryu, goju-ryu and wado-ryu (see Main karate styles, page 10). Though they differ in technique, in essence they have remained the same. Each requires hard work and discipline, and no one style is any better or worse than another.

During the Second World War, European and American servicemen were sent to Japan and Okinawa, and many of them began to practise this new fighting art. When the war finished, these new recruits took what they had learnt back to their respective countries, thus helping to spread the sport worldwide.

But, because of the various different styles, karate competition proved difficult, if not impossible. So in 1964 the Japanese government initiated the formation of the All Japan Karate-do Federation (FAJKO), which incorporated all the major clubs.

However, progress elsewhere was slow, and it took several years for other countries to follow suit and organize their own national federations.

In 1970 the first 'all styles' world championships were held in Tokyo, and at the same time the World Union of Karate-do Organizations (WUKO) was set up to govern the sport around the world. Ten years later women first started competing at the Championships.

Unsurprisingly, Japan was the first winner of the world championships, which are now held every two years. But it was not long before other nations began to compete at the same level. Great Britain in particular has had a great deal of success, with fighters such as Vic Charles and Jeoff Thompson leading from the front.

The world karate championships, 1992.

Main karate styles

Shotokan: The first style to be popularized in Japan, it was created in 1922 by Gichin Funakoshi. This very powerful style originated on the island of Okinawa and now has the largest following around the world. Competition is not stressed, but when it takes place it is tough and uncompromising.

Shito-ryu: This was established in 1930 by Kenwa Mabuni, who also hailed from Okinawa. Because it incorporates the principle characteristics of all the other methods, it involves a wide range of katas (see page 43). It is widely used in competitions around the world, though this has not affected its traditional movements.

Goju-ryu: A few years after Mabuni, Okinawan Chojun Miyagi brought the goju-ryu form of karate to Japan. This is a very traditional style that involves little competition. There are few katas to learn, and it is noted for the special training exercises used to build bodily strength.

Wado-ryu: Known as the 'way of peace', this was created in 1935 by Hironori Ohtsuka, one of Funakoshi's most senior students. It uses many evasion techniques, which bear a strong resemblance to some ju-jitsu methods, as Ohtsuka was already a ju-jitsu master. Ohtsuka was also the first to pioneer competition karate.

GETTING STARTED

Choosing the right club

It is very important that you begin your karate career in the proper way, and to do that you must choose the right club. If you make the mistake of picking the wrong one, you could waste many years of hard work and practice.

Selecting the correct club is not as easy as it sounds. There are no set rules governing the formation of karate clubs, and it has been known for students without the necessary qualifications to start up on their own. So you must be very careful before you make your decision.

Here are a few simple guidelines:

○ Look at all the clubs in your area – do not automatically choose the first one. Only by looking at several will you be able to make an informed decision.

○ Watch the training sessions – if the club is established it will have students who have reached a high standard. If you cannot see any brown or black belts, the chances are it has been going only a couple of years.

 Competitive karate takes place on a safety mat, which has markings indicating where competitors must stand before and after a contest.

○ See if it is recognized by an official body and has a licence to teach. In England, for example, the English Karate Governing Body oversees the sport, and licences are issued on its behalf by the individual karate authorities.

○ Make sure your membership fee includes a personal accident insurance policy. This will protect you if you suffer an injury or accidentally injure somebody else.

Equipment

Uniform: Karate students, otherwise called karateka, wear a white training uniform known as the karategi. After your first few lessons, if you have decided to take the sport seriously, you must purchase a karategi.

The karategi should be loose-fitting so that it does not restrict you in any way. The jacket must be long enough to cover your hips, and female students should wear a plain white T-shirt or a sports bra underneath. The sleeves should come halfway down the forearm, and the legs of the trousers must cover two-thirds of the shin.

Try to keep your karategi clean and in good condition, as this shows a correct attitude to training. When you buy a new one, make sure it is a size too big. Suits always shrink in the wash, and it is better to have one that is too big at first than one that is too small after a month of washing! Ask your club where you can purchase one. A lot of clubs sell suits, and it is often less expensive than buying one from a shop.

A pair of flip-flops or sandals are always useful, as they will help to keep your feet warm and clean when you are not on the training mat.

Belts: Karategi come with a standard white belt. Like other martial arts, karate has an assessment method known as 'grading examinations'. These can be taken after every forty-eight hours of training, and allow the student and instructor to see how the student is improving.

Each grade is indicated with a different-coloured belt. Coloured stages are known as kyu (student) grades, and the black belt is known as the dan (senior) grade. The colours of the belt vary depending on the karate style, but the most common scheme is:

White	–	novice grade
Red	–	6th kyu
Yellow	–	5th kyu
Orange	–	4th kyu
Green	–	3rd kyu
Blue	–	2nd kyu
Brown	–	1st kyu
Black	–	1st dan.

There is a correct way of tying a karate belt, and your instructor, or a more experienced student, will show you how it is done.

Protection

Because karate is a contact sport, there is always a danger you may get injured. There are a number of items that will help to avoid injury.

Padded gloves: White regulation mitts will help to protect your hands and your opponent should you accidentally make too much contact. The padding should be no more than

Adopting the correct stance shows a keen willingness to learn, as well as respect for the class.

1 cm thick, and the thumb must be left free.

Gumshield: If you should receive a blow to the mouth, the gumshield will absorb the shock and help to protect your teeth and jaw.

Jockstrap: This is vital for males and will help to protect and support your most vulnerable parts.

When you begin to spar at a higher level, there are several other protective items you may want to use. Males should buy a 'box' or 'groin protector', while chest, instep and shin protectors are also a good idea. For students with long hair, a sweatband is a must – if your hair keeps getting in your eyes it will distract you enormously!

Etiquette

A good karate club will stress the importance or etiquette within the dojo (the training hall). It is often said that: 'karate begins and ends with courtesy', and you should always bear this in mind.

Be polite and courteous to your instructor and senior students at all times. Remember, they were once at your level, and have progressed only through their own hard work, determination and discipline.

There are a couple of simple bows and instructions you must follow to show respect to your karate school, your instructor and fellow students.

Rei: This is the ritual bow which must be observed when you enter the dojo, and before and after training with a partner. Keep your feet together and your hands by your side. The

When performing the ritual bow (Rei), make the movement smooth and remember to pause momentarily when you reach the lowest point.

After a karate lesson, you will be instructed to perform a bow (Seiza) as a sign of respect for your teacher.

movement should be smooth and unhurried, with a slight pause at the lowest point.

If your teacher or other senior students are present when you enter the dojo, direct your bow toward them.

Seiza: This bow is used to show respect for your teacher. When you hear the order 'seiza', squat down with your knees open. Lower your weight on to your left knee first and then your right, and reverse the sequence when rising. Remember to keep your back straight and your hands positioned above your knees.

On the second command of 'sensei ni rei', slide your hands forward and perform a gradual bow. Keep your head up so you can see your instructor, and once again pause momentarily at the lowest point.

When you hear the command 'kiritsu', the class should rise. Lift your right knee first, then your left, and straighten into a standing position with your heels together.

Fitness for karate

As with most sports, it is vital to maintain a good level of fitness for karate. To realize your potential it is important for your body to be in good shape. During karate training you will be using your legs, arms and

Competition area
A competition mat measures 8 m by 8 m, with a 1 m safety area around the perimeter. It is made up of smaller mats laid together, which should never be allowed to come apart. There are two markers in the middle indicating where the opponents must stand at the start or restart of a contest.

GO FOR SPORT!: KARATE

body in a way you may not be used to, and if your fitness is below par you will find it difficult to manage. What's more, you may get an injury and put yourself out of action for a while.

Most karate clubs will expect you to train two or three times a week, and during these sessions time will be put aside for fitness. Here we will concentrate on a few basic exercises you can do on your own to help your overall fitness and agility.

Warm-up and stretching

A good warm-up prepares your body for the training session ahead. It is now recognized as one of the most vital aspects of a sportsman or sportswoman's fitness regime. This is especially true of karate, which requires a high degree of suppleness.

It is important to stretch the main parts of your body.

A Hamstring and calf stretch.
B Neck stretch.
C Shoulder stretch.
D Groin stretch.

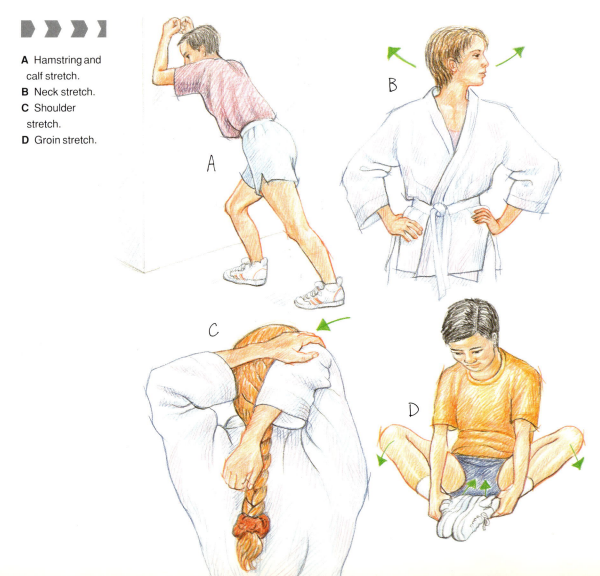

A Hamstring and calf stretch: Push hard against a wall, keeping your back leg straight and your front knee bent. Your back heel should remain firmly pressed against the floor. Change legs.

B Neck stretch: With your shoulders relaxed and hands on your hips, move your head to each side in slow, deliberate movements. Repeat several times before doing the same in an up-and-down direction.

C Shoulder stretch: Bend your elbow and move one of your arms to the side of your head. Take your elbow in your other hand and gently draw it back behind your head. Repeat this a number of times and then change arms.

D Groin stretch: Sit on the floor, with your legs bent and the soles of your feet touching. Hold your ankles and gradually pull your feet toward your groin. At the same time, gently push your knees down.

These are just some of the simple stretching exercises that will help your flexibility. Remember, try to make the movements slow and purposeful, not jerky. There will come a point when the exercise starts to hurt. Try always to reach this point gradually, then hold your position for a second or two before relaxing.

It is also important to 'warm down' after a training session, as this helps to prevent muscles from stiffening up. Use these exercises for this purpose as well.

Fitness training

In addition to exercises for warming up and increasing flexibility, there are those which you must do to improve strength and power. The following will help to work some of the main muscles you will use in training.

Press-ups: These are for your arms, shoulders, elbows and upper body. Place your palms flat on the floor and, with your back straight, lower yourself down before pushing up to the start position. This exercise can be varied by moving your hands closer together and pointing your palms inward.

Burpees: These develop the muscles in your arms and legs. From a standing position, drop into a crouch, and thrust both your legs backward. Bring them back to the crouch position, before standing up once again.

GO FOR SPORT!: KARATE

Sit-ups: For your stomach and upper leg muscles, lie on your back, with knees bent and both hands behind your head. Raise your body until your head reaches your knees. Return halfway and repeat.

Dorsal raises: For the muscles in your back and buttocks, lie on your tummy with your hands behind your head. Raise your head and legs as far as you can at the same time, before returning to the original position.

Karate training also requires a great deal of stamina, which depends on the amount of oxygen our lungs can inhale in order to feed the muscles being used. This is called 'aerobic capacity'. Jogging, cycling, swimming and aerobics are all good exercises to help build stamina.

Competitive karate requires a high level of physical fitness – a good training routine will help you to achieve this.

TECHNIQUES 1

Points of contact

Karate is a contact sport, and certain parts of your body must be used for striking, kicking and sweeping your opponent. Before we move on to the basic techniques, it is important for you to know exactly which parts to use.

Forefist (seiken): Contact is made with the knuckles of the first and middle fingers. Bend your fingers into your palms, and fold your thumb across the first two. Never tuck your thumb under your fingers, as you could easily break it this way. The tighter the fist the better, as this will help to protect your wrist.

Backfist (uraken): The backfist is used for making contact with an opponent's temple or nose. Make the same fist as before, but this time contact is made with the back of the two large knuckles.

Single-knuckle fist (ippon ken): Extend the middle finger of your fist so that the middle knuckle is slightly raised. Contact should be made with this knuckle.

Knifehand (shuto): This is for chopping and blocking. Your thumb must be locked across your palm to avoid it getting injured.

Spearhand (nukite): The spearhand is for attacking the soft parts of your opponent's body. Make the same hand as before, but force your thumb even further across your palm. Contact is made with the middle three fingers.

Elbow (empi): For close-in attacks, the elbow can be used to strike from all directions.

Knee (hiza): This is useful for close-in attacks on your opponent's stomach.

Heel (kakato): This is used when performing backward kicks.

Instep (haisoku): The instep is mainly used for kicks to the head. Contact should be made just in front of the ankle. Be careful not to strike with your toes, as this can be very painful.

Ball of the foot (chusoko): This is used in front kicks and roundhouse kicks. Contact is made with the thick pad of flesh that runs beneath your toes.

Foot edge (sokuto): The outside edge of your foot is used mainly for side-kicks.

Stances

In order to perform the various karate techniques, it is vital that your body starts from the correct

From the ready stance, a karateka is prepared for immediate action.

With most of the weight on your front foot, the forward stance allows you to perform strong, powerful punches.

position. Stances are very important, as they enable you to put maximum power behind your punches, strikes and kicks. Adopting the right stance will also assist your evasion techniques.

There are a number of basic stances.

Ready stance (shizentai): This prepares you for imminent action. Your feet should be shoulder-width apart, and your fists clenched by your sides.

Front stance (zenkutsu dachi): This is a strong, attacking stance. With most of your body weight over your front leg, it prepares you for powerful punches.

Back stance (kokutsu dachi): The back stance is used in defence and mainly for blocking frontal attacks. Put most of your weight on your back leg, which should be sharply bent and with the toes at a ninety-degree angle to your front foot.

Fighting stance (hanmei gamae): From the back stance, move your body weight forward so there is a fifty-fifty distribution over both legs. Move your front foot slightly outward to give you balance on each side. The purpose of this stance is to allow you to make forward or backward movements, depending on what the situation demands.

From the fighting stance, you should be ready to move forward or backwards, depending on what is required.

GO FOR SPORT!: KARATE

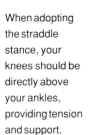

When adopting the straddle stance, your knees should be directly above your ankles, providing tension and support.

Straddle stance (shiko dachi): From the ready stance, move your left foot outward to the side, and then your right foot. Rotate your feet outward slightly, but make sure your knees are directly above your ankles. The stance provides tension and support. With the toes turned slightly inward this is called kiba dachi.

Cat stance (neko ashi dachi): Most of your body weight should be on the back leg, with your front foot posed and ready for kicking.

TECHNIQUES 2

Punches

Now that you are aware which parts of the body are designated for contact and how to adopt the correct stances, we can move on to some of the basic punches and strikes.

Remember never to fully extend your arms when punching, or your legs when kicking, as this may cause joint problems later in life.

Straight punch (choku zuki): This is the most basic karate punch, and is performed from the 'ready' stance.

The punching hand should begin at the waist and travel in a straight line to your target. Keep your hand and body relaxed until just before contact. Twist your hand 180 degrees and make contact with your forefist. At the same time your other arm should travel in the opposite direction.

Lunge punch (oi zuki): This is very similar to the straight punch, except that it incorporates a step forward or backward. Start from the 'forward' stance, with your left leg leading and your left arm extended. Drive off your rear foot and, just as you begin to put

◄◄◄◄

When performing a straight punch, your punching arm should travel in a straight line to its target...

▼▼▼▼

...Directing a punch in a contest is much more difficult!

weight on your front foot, pull back your left arm and punch with your right.

Timing of the punch is critical, as it must land while the body is still moving. That way power is gained from your momentum, as well as from the snapping action of your arms. At this point your hips should be square on and your body tensed. If the punch lands too early it can easily put you off balance.

As you progress, you will have to perform a series of lunge punches, moving from leg to leg alternately. Getting the step right is difficult, and at first you will probably find the gap between your feet widening or narrowing. Always try to keep your knees bent, as this should prevent you from bobbing up and down, thus losing balance and power.

Snap punch (kizami zuki): This is very similar to the jab in boxing, and relies more on the element of suprise than on the power of the punch. It is different from the lunge punch because you do not alter your stance. Deliver the punch at speed, and you will find it useful for opening up your opponent's defence.

Reverse punch (gyaku zuki): This is similar to the lunge punch, except that in this case your opposite arm and leg are used to lead. It is possibly karate's strongest punch, with power generated from bringing your back leg to the front and twisting your hips sharply.

Begin by performing the punch on the spot from the left forward stance, with your left hand positioned just above your knee. When your right hand comes through, withdraw your left arm simultaneously. As your right hand turns over to punch, remember

A snap punch is like a boxer's jab, and relies on the element of surprise.

GO FOR SPORT!: KARATE

▶▶▶

The reverse punch is the most powerful punch in karate. Power is generated by bringing your back leg forward and twisting your hips.

to thrust your right hip forward, and this will enable you to put power behind the move.

Extra power can now be added by including a step. From the same stance, bring your right leg forward, so that it slips past your left. Transfer your weight in the usual way, keeping your height constant throughout the step. As you approach your new stance, pull back your leading arm and deliver the punch through a straight line with your left fist. Again, remember to drive forward with your left hip.

It is important to make sure your stance is correct when you deliver the punch, because if you are too high you will lose some of the force. Also, try to keep your shoulders relaxed. If they are hunched, your

GO FOR SPORT!: KARATE

▼▼▼

Like the snap punch, a back fist must be performed at speed and contact is made with the back of your fist.

upper body will be forced back when you make contact with your target.

Remember the following points when delivering a reverse punch:

○ Keep your height constant when making the step.

○ In stepping forward, make sure your rear leg brushes past your front leg.

○ Drive your hip forward.

○ Keep your shoulders relaxed.

Backfist (uraken): This is similar to the front jab, but this time it is delivered with the back of the fist. Begin in the forward stance, and bring your front hand back toward your jaw. Your arm should then spring out and the back of your fist should make contact with the side of your opponent's face. Remember to keep your elbow up, as this will allow you to get the necessary snapping action for the punch.

Kicks

As well as your fists, the other main weapons you have at your disposal are your feet. Basically, there are three types of kick:

❍ Snap-kicks, which rely on snapping the leg forward and back, as quickly as possible.

❍ Thrust-kicks, which are used to generate power– the knee is always raised before the leg is thrust forward in a straight action.

❍ Strike-kicks, which are used for blocking and attacking, and rely mainly on flexibility.

In this book we will deal only with the first two. With every kick you learn, remember that balance is a key factor. You must always keep the sole of your non-kicking foot firmly on the ground, as this will increase your stability.

Front kick (mae geri): This is a snap-kick, and the ball of your foot should make contact with your opponent's stomach or chin. The power comes from your hips and from the snapping action of the kicking leg.

From the forward stance, lift your back foot off the floor and bring your knee upward and forward in the centre of your body. As the knee reaches the correct height, straighten the lower part of your leg, and thrust your hips forward. Your instep must be straightened and your toes should be bent backwards, otherwise they might be injured. After making contact, withdraw your leg to the original position.

It is vital to maintain your balance, and this is aided by turning your grounded foot slightly outward when raising your knee. Also, make sure the action is smooth and continuous – if the movement is jerky you will

The front kick.

GO FOR SPORT!: KARATE

lose speed, momentum and power.
Remember the following points:

○   Make sure your knee is brought up to the correct height.

○   Keep your kicking leg in the centre of your body.

○   Withdraw your kicking leg as soon as contact is made.

○   Unless practising against a bag, never fully straighten your kicking leg, as this may damage the knee joint.

Back kick (ushiro geri): Regarded as one of the most powerful thrust-kicks in karate, it relies on the pivoting effect of your hips and upper body.

The best way to learn the back kick is to start from a position where you have your back to your opponent. Lift your rear knee up toward the front, before driving it out parallel to the floor. Keep the toes of your foot pointing downward, and thrust the heel of your foot into your opponent's target area.

Once you feel comfortable performing the kick from this position, move your body so it is at a ninety-degree angle to your opponent, before trying the kick again. This time, swivel your body round so that you are facing away from your opponent once again, and then deliver the back kick straight toward your opponent.

Finally, you should learn how to deliver the kick from a position facing your opponent. From the left fighting stance, turn your body through 180 degrees, raising your right knee at the same time.

 Keeping your body balanced is crucial when performing any kicking technique.

GO FOR SPORT!: KARATE

As soon as you are facing the opposite direction, thrust your right leg out and deliver the back kick. You should be able to generate power from the rotating movement of your body and from your hips.

Once you have made contact, bring your leg back to the bent knee position, and twist your body round so that you are once again facing your opponent.

Try to remember the following points:

◯ Keep your eyes on your opponent at all times.

◯ The kick must be delivered in a straight, backward line.

◯ Keep your toes pointed down, and strike with your heel.

Roundhouse kick (mawashi geri): Like the front kick, the roundhouse kick relies on power and flexibility from the hips. The aim is to kick round your opponent's guard with your instep, making contact with either the side of his or her body or the side of the head.

Bring your knee up and to the side, keeping your leg bent and your toes

A roundhouse kick is designed to kick round your opponent's guard, with your instep making contact with the side of his or her head or body.

GO FOR SPORT!: KARATE

curled. Once the leg is in the correct position, snap it forward into your opponent's target area, before returning it to the original position.

Again, this kick requires great balance, so your upper body should be almost at right angles to your supporting leg. Your knee must be raised to a sufficient height before you deliver the kick.

Side kick (yoko geri): This is a thrust-kick, with the power going sideways from the body.

From the straddle stance, slide your rear leg forward, bringing your front foot off the floor at the same time. Raise your knee to about waist

The roundhouse kick.

Your supporting leg must provide maximum balance and support while performing a side kick.

GO FOR SPORT!: KARATE

Keep your eyes on your opponent when you perform a back kick.

height, and turn your body sideways so that it is at a ninety-degree angle to your opponent. Extend your leg and thrust it out sideways into your opponent's stomach or chest, using the heel or side of your foot to make contact.

Once contact has been made, withdraw your leg immediately. Again you must bend the knee before returning your foot to the floor. Failure to do this in one motion will leave you open to a counter-attack.

The side kick requires excellent balance, which should come from the ball of your grounded foot and supporting leg.

Remember the following points:

○ Raise your knee to the correct height before driving your leg sideways.

○ Keep facing your opponent so that you can always keep him or her in view.

○ Withdraw your leg immediately once contact is made.

TECHNIQUES 3

Blocking

Having learnt the fundamental karate kicks and punches, it is important to know how to defend yourself when your opponent uses these attacking moves against you.

A block is a defensive technique that diverts an attack, often using the minimum of force. This way a person can successfully defend himself or herself against a larger and more powerful opponent.

Blocking can also be a way of turning your opponent's force to your advantage. If you successfully manage to divert an attack, you can throw your opponent off balance and follow up with a counter-attack of your own.

Some karateka can defend themselves by making a blow to an attacking limb, while others will merely deflect the attack. Here we will concentrate on deflection.

There are three rules of thumb:
◯ Attacks to the head must be deflected upwards.
◯ Attacks to the upper body must be deflected sideways.

 Taking evasive action is one way of dealing with an attack, but blocks can be the basis of a counter-attack.

An upper block is used to deflect attacks to your head.

◯ Attacks to the lower body must be deflected downward.

There are four basic blocks.

Upper block (age uke): This is used to defend an attack to your head. When you think your opponent is about to deliver the punch, bring your forward arm back and then up, so that the underside of your forearm faces your opponent. If your arm is brought up in the correct arc, the outer side of your forearm should

GO FOR SPORT!: KARATE

make contact with the underneath of your attacker's wrist, and deflect the punch away.

It is important to keep the elbow of your deflecting arm lower than your fist, as well as in line with the front of your body. Otherwise your defence will be weakened.

If the block is completed successfully, your opponent will lose balance and be left open to a counter-attack.

Outside arm block (soto ude uke): This involves a sweeping movement of your arm to deflect attacks to your chest. Contact is made between the fleshy bit of your forearm and your opponent's attacking arm, just above the wrist. It is called the 'outside' arm block because your arm travels from outside your body, and contact is made with the outside of your opponent's arm.

From a forward stance, bring your

The outside arm block parries attacks to your chest, using a sweeping movement of your arm travelling from outside your body.

rear arm well back and then across the front of your body in a semicircular motion. Just prior to contact, turn your wrist round 180 degrees so that your forearm parries the attack sideways.

Again, if this move is performed well, your opponent will be left open to a counter-attack.

Inside arm block (uchi ude uke): Again, this block is used to defend against attacks to your chest. It is easier for beginners to master and is called the 'inside' arm block because your arm moves from inside the area of your body.

It involves moving your arm in an arc across your body, with fist clenched. Use the thumb side of your forearm to make contact with the inside of your opponent's arm and deflect the attack.

This block should be used when there is insufficient space or time to

 An inside arm block is used when you have minimum time or space to deflect an opponent's attack.

GO FOR SPORT!: KARATE

The downward arm block is an effective means of defence against punches or kicks to your body.

perform an outside arm block. It is particularly effective against opponents who have a tendency to swing their punches rather than drive them straight.

Downward block (gedan barai): This is the most basic of all blocks, and is used more than any other blocking techniques. It is the main defence for attacks aimed at your stomach.

From the ready stance, move your left foot forward and bring your left arm back so that your fist is just above your right shoulder. Pull your right arm back so it is just above the waist, and at the same time straighten your left arm. It should move in a downward direction to meet the oncoming attack.

It is possible to use either your left or your right arm to perform this block. But as most people are right-handed, they tend to favour their left, as this then leaves your stronger right arm

GO FOR SPORT!: KARATE

free for counter-attacks.

When using the downward block against a punch, force can be met with force. However, when used against a front kick, the block must be more of a deflection. This is because an opponent's leg is obviously stronger than your arm, and you do not want to injure yourself in the block.

Combinations

Having learnt some of the fundamental karate techniques, we can now look at combining these into a series of punches and kicks. Single punches or kicks can be easily blocked, but if they are performed in a combination it makes

 Follow up a snap punch with a reverse punch.

it harder for your opponent to defend against.

The easiest combination to perform is a block and counter-punch. Here we will concentrate on a couple of other basic combinations.

Front kick/Reverse punch: From a left fighting stance, start with a right front kick to your opponent's stomach. As you set your leg down, and transfer your weight, pull back your right arm and deliver a reverse punch with your left. Remember to twist your hips forward to give maximum power to the punch.

Snap punch/Reverse punch/ Roundhouse kick: This is a little more complicated than the first, as it involves combining three basic techniques.

From the left fighting stance, step into the right fighting stance and snap a right-handed punch to your opponent's face. Pull back the arm and follow through with a strong left-handed reverse punch to his or her chest.

As you pull back the punch, swing your left hip round and deliver a left-footed roundhouse kick to the head.

It is important you complete each part of a combination before moving on to the next. Most beginners make the mistake of concentrating on the final move, and therefore fail to perform the whole combination correctly.

At first your instructor will select combinations for you to practise, and will choose techniques that naturally follow on from each other. As you become more experienced, these combinations will get more complicated and difficult, and after a while you should be able to develop some of your own.

Sparring

In modern-day karate, sparring plays a major role. Karate is now a recognized sport world-wide, and the 'fighting' aspects allow karateka to test their skills and techniques against each other. This side of the sport is called kumite.

Beginners should not be allowed to spar, and your club will insist you wait until you have a good understanding of all the basic techniques. Kumite can be dangerous, and therefore those taking part must be experienced and responsible.

Some karateka enjoy sparring, while others would rather concentrate on the karate patterns (see Kata, page 43). However, sparring is an important part of training, so you should be prepared for it at some stage of your karate career.

Sparring basically involves practising techniques against someone of similar height and size. It is often an advantage to spar with someone more experienced. He or she will have more control over movements, and therefore the chances of getting injured are reduced.

The aim of sparring is not to 'bash up' your opponent. As you know, there are designated targets on your opponent's body, and you must take care when attacking them. When aiming for the face, close your hands fully. With every kick, punch and strike, the power must be controlled. The intention is to practise, not to injure.

Competition

Competitive karate is the next step up from sparring, and is purely optional. Competitors fight on an 8 m x 8 m mat (see Equipment, page 12), and the bout is controlled by a referee. One fighter wears a red belt, and is known as aka, the other wears a white belt and is known as shiro. This helps the referee, who awards points throughout the match, to tell them apart.

There are two marks on the mat showing each fighter where to stand at the beginning of a bout. The contestants must bow to each other before the match commences. It begins with the referee shouting 'shobusanbon hajime'. When he or she wants to halt the bout, or bring it to a close, he or she shouts 'yame'.

During the match the referee is assisted by a judge, and an arbitrator keeps a note of the scores as they are awarded. A scorer keeps an official record of scores in the competition, while a timekeeper stops and starts the bouts in accordance with the rules.

The winner is the competitor with the most points at the end of a bout, or the first to reach one or three points. Whole points, known as ippons, are awarded for clean and successful attacks. For attacks which are not quite perfect, half a point, or waza-ari, is awarded. When an attack

GO FOR SPORT!: KARATE

Competitive karate allows karateka to test their skills and fitness against opponents of similar size and experience. A referee awards points for clean and successful attacks and deducts points for incorrect technique.

is successful, the referee temporarily stops the bout to award a score.

The referee warns a fighter if he or she breaks the rules of competition. Points are deducted if a competitor repeats an offence, and for serious infringements, such as attacking prohibited areas of the body or using forbidden techniques. The referee uses a variety of signals to indicate the scoring and awarding of points.

Once again the aim is not to hurt or injure your opponent. You must stay composed and your attacks must be controlled. Contact is essential, but too much contact will lead to you losing points.

Kata

There is no literal translation for kata in the English language, but the closest meaning is 'pattern'. The word is used to describe a sequence of moves, blocks and counter-attacks which are performed against an imaginary opponent.

Before the formation of 'free

GO FOR SPORT!: KARATE

▶▶▶▶ For karateka who do not wish to spar, kata is an excellent way of expressing karate skills and requires great stamina and concentration.

sparring', kata was the best way for karateka to express themselves, as it requires stamina, flexibility and total concentration of mind and bodily movements. The katas practised today have evolved over hundreds of years. They represent the traditional aspects of karate that have stood the test of time.

Because kata is an excellent way of practising techniques and moves, students are introduced to this aspect of karate at an early stage in their careers. In shotokan, the early katas are called heians, and most of them begin with a defensive movement. In all the various styles, there are about fifty different katas, while shotokan has some twenty-six or twenty-seven.

Kata cannot be practised too much. At first you will have to pay attention to remembering the various stages of the pattern, but after a while they become automatic. You can then concentrate on technique and the true meaning of the kata, as each movement has a purpose. As you progress, the katas become more and more difficult.

To become a successful karateka, you will have to master a range of katas. Many students prefer this aspect to kumite, and enter kata competitions as opposed to free sparring events. In these competitions you are marked on the technical merit of your kata, as well as on etiquette.

Karate is a martial art which goes back several centuries, and as a beginner you should be aware of the traditions that have developed over the years. Karate is based on self-discipline and respect. You must be fit and flexible to get the most out of it, and you should be prepared for the commitment it requires.

Remember that karate originated as a means of self-defence. Learning karate will give you the ability to look after yourself in unarmed combat, but this does not mean you should go looking for trouble. Always try to avoid conflict.

The important thing is for you to enjoy yourself in the true spirit of karate. At first, many of its moves and customs will appear alien to you, and this is to be expected. However, after a while you will become accustomed to its ways, and as your technique and fitness progress, you will gain a great deal of satisfaction from this ancient art form. So don't hold back – go for karate!

Glossary

Age uke Upper block.
Age zuki Rising punch.
Bari Block.
Choku zuki Straight punch.
Chudan Mid-level of body.
Chusoko Ball of the foot.
Dachi Stance.
Dan Level of black belt grade.
Do The way of.
Dojo Training hall.
Empi Elbow.
Empi uchi Elbow strike.
Gedan Lower body.
Gedan bari Lower block.
Gedan zuki Lower punch.
Geri Kick.
Gi Training outfit.
Goju-ryu Karate style.
Gyaku Reverse.
Gyaku zuki Reverse punch.
Haisoku Instep.
Haito Ridge hand.
Hanmei gamae Fighting stance.
Heisoku dachi Feet-together stance.
Hiza Knee.
Hiza geri Knee kick.
Ippon Whole point.
Ippon ken Single-knuckle fist.
Jiu kumite Free sparring.
Jodan Upper body.
Jodan uke Upper body block.
Jodan zuki Punch to the upper body.

Kakato Heel.
Kara-te Empty hands/China hands.
Karateka Karate student.
Kata Training sequence.
Keri (Geri) Kick.
Kiai Karate shout.
Kiba dachi Straddle stance.
Kime Focus.
Kizami zuki Snap punch.
Kokutsu dachi Back stance.
Koshi Ball of the foot.
Kumite Sparring.
Mae geri Front kick.
Makiwara Striking post.
Mawashi geri Roundhouse kick.
Mawashi zuki Roundhouse punch.
Neko ashi dachi Cat stance.
Nukite Spearhand.
Nunchaku Rice flail used as karate weapon.
Oi zuki Lunge punch.
Rei Bow.
Ryu School.
Seiken Forefist.
Seiza Kneeling position/Bow.
Sempai Senior.
Sensei Teacher.
Shihan Master.
Shiko dachi Straddle stance.
Shiro White belt in competition.

Shito-ryu Karate style.
Shizentai Ready stance.
Shobun Competition.
Shotokan Karate style.
Shuto Knifehand.
Sokuto Foot edge.
Soto ude uke Outside arm block.
Tameshiwari Wood-breaking.
Te Hand.
Tekubi Wrist.
Tsukite Punching hand.
Uchi Strike.
Uchi ude uke Inside arm block.
Ude Forearm.
Uke Block.
Uraken Backfist.
Ushiro geri Back kick.
Wado-ryu Karate style.
Waza-ari Half point in competition.
Yame Stop.
Yoi Ready.
Yoko Side.
Yoko geri Side kick.
Zenkutsu dachi Forward stance.
Zuki Punch.

Further reading

The Beginner's Guide To Shotokan Karate by John Van Weenen (Paul Hooley Associates, 1983)
Beginning Karate by David Mitchell (Bowerden Press, 1987)
Karate Basic Manual by A. Pfluger (Sterling Publishing Co., 1982)
Karate – The Pursuit of Excellence by Jeoff Thompson (Ward Lock, 1988)
Play the Game – Karate by Karl Oldgate (Ward Lock, 1990)
Step by Step Karate Skills by Dan Bradley (Hamlyn, 1987)
Traditional Karate by Ticky Donovan (Penguin, 1989)

Useful Addresses

English Karate Governing Body
M. Dinsdale
12 Princes Avenue
Woodford Green
Essex IG8 OLN
England

Irish National Karate Association
J. Booth
12 North Frederick Street
Dublin 1
Irish Republic

Northern Ireland Karate Board
M. Leyden
33 Corrina Park
Upper Dunmurry
Dunmurry
Northern Ireland

Welsh Karate Federation
Mrs Mumberson
Smalldrink
Parsonage Lane
Begelly
Kilgetty
Dyfed
Wales

Scottish Karate Board
A. Murdoch
48 Ryde Road
Wishaw ML2 7DX
Scotland

World Union of Karate-do Organizations
Senpaku Sinko Building
1-15-16 Toranoman
Minatu-Ku
Tokyo 105
Japan

Index

Numbers in **bold** refer to captions.

All Japanese Karate-do
    Federation (FAJKO)   9
'all styles' world championships
    9
    women competing in   9

belts   11, 12, 13
blocking   35
    downward block   39, 40
    inside arm block   38, 39
    outside arm block   37, 38, 39
    upper block   36, 37
bowing   14, 15

Charles, Vic   **7**, 9
China   7, 8
clubs   11-12
combinations   40-41
competition karate   4, 8, 15, 42, 43, 45
counter-attack   34, 35, 37, 38

dan   12, 13
discipline   5, 8

English Karate Governing Body   12
equipment   12-14
    protective   13, 14
etiquette   14-15

fitness   4, 15, 16, 45
    training   16, 17, 18
forefist   19, 24
Funakoshi, Gichin   8

Great Britain   9

history   6-10

India   7

Japan   7, 8, 9, 10

kata   10, 43-45
kicks
    back   30, 31, 32
    front   29, 30, 32
    roundhouse   32, 33
    side   33, 34
kyu grades   12, 13

Mabuni, Kenwa   10
main karate styles
    goju-ryu   8, 10
    shito-ryu   8, 10
    shotokan   4, 8,10, 45
    wado-ryu   8, 10
Miyagi, Chojun   10

Ohtsuka, Hironori   10
Okinawa   7, 8, 10
Okinawa-te   8

points of contact   19-20
punches
    backfist   19, 28
    lunge   24, 25, 26
    reverse   26, 27,28, 41
    snap   26
    straight   24, 25

scoring   42, 43
Second World War   8
Shaolin monastery   7
sparring   41, 42
    'free'   43, 44, 45
stances
    back   22

cat   23
fighting   22, 41
front   21, 26, 28, 29
ready   21, 23, 24, 39
straddle   23, 33

Thompson, Jeoff   9

warming-up   16-17
World Union of Karate-do
    Organizations (WUKO)   9

96-027

796.8
ORO
O'Rorke, Terence.
Karate

SAM SHERRATT PUBLIC SCHOOL
649 LAURIER AVENUE
MILTON, ONTARIO
L9T 4N4